IN CASE OF LOSS, PLEASE RETURN TO:

Name: _____

Address: _____

City: _____

State: _____ Zip Code: _____

Country: _____

HOW TO PACK

Published in the United States by
Clarkson Potter/Publishers, an imprint of
the Crown Publishing Group, a division of
Penguin Random House LLC, New York.
crownpublishing.com
clarksonpotter.com

CLARKSON POTTER is a trademark
and POTTER with colophon is a registered
trademark of Penguin Random House LLC.

Library of Congress Cataloging-in-
Publication Data
Names: Palepu, Hitha, author.
Title: How to pack : travel smart for any
trip / Hitha Palepu.
Description: New York : Clarkson Potter,
2017.
Identifiers: LCCN 2016009740| ISBN
9781101905647 (print : alk. paper) | ISBN
9780553459876 (ebook)
Subjects: LCSH: Travel—Handbooks,
manuals, etc. |
  Luggage—Packing—Handbooks,
manuals, etc.
Classification: LCC G151 .P34 2017 |
DDC 646/.6—dc23 LC record available at
https://lccn.loc.gov/2016009740

ISBN 978-1-101-90564-7
eBook ISBN 978-0-553-45987-6

Printed in China

Book and cover design by Ian Dingman
Art by Kelly Lasserre

10 9 8 7 6 5 4 3 2 1

First Edition

HOW TO PACK

Travel Smart for Any Trip

HITHA PALEPU

Illustrated by Kelly Lasserre

CLARKSON POTTER/PUBLISHERS
NEW YORK

CONTENTS

Preparing for Takeoff

HOW TO PRE-PACK 19

Ready to Wear

CHOOSING CLOTHES
WITH STYLE 37

Secret Weapons

THE RIGHT ACCESSORIES
CAN MAKE YOUR LOOK 53

Pack Pretty

Putting It All Together

Come Fly with Me

Introduction

I'm the kind of person who always likes the journey as much as the destination. The first flight I can remember taking was when I was six years old. I traveled to India with my mother. I'd been there to visit my family before, but had only hazy memories of our previous visits—the expansive terrace atop my grandparents' house, brightly colored paper kites flying above, the small balls of rice and lentils my aunt fed me while telling me the more obscure (and entertaining!) stories of Hindu mythology. My sharpest memory, however, is of the luggage we brought on the trip. The week before our departure, my mother laid open four mammoth suitcases in our living room. In went rolls of toilet paper, giant bags of candy, piles of shirts. A new Teflon-coated pan sat next to a frilly dress intended for my cousin. As we got closer to our departure date, the suitcases were filled with gifts for everyone.

I imagined the suitcases were indestructible, but in reality their heavy weight and the rough handling of the journey left them in tatters, patched with shiny, bright red-and-green Air India stickers and coarse string. The gifts, however, arrived in perfect condition. The family chef put her new pan to work straightaway, frying up my favorite spiced potatoes. My cousin beamed when she saw the dress and immediately tried it on, twirling around the room. The pure joy on my mother's face, however, is what stayed with me. The shopping trips, the long hours spent packing—it was all worth it. *You are what you pack* was the first travel lesson I learned. My mother, being the most generous person I know, always packed for others and never for herself.

I, on the other hand, have always packed for the person I want to be. As a kid, my first in-flight bags were filled with books, a fresh journal, and a new set of pencils to create a world for myself as the artist I felt I was. When I packed for our move from Pennsylvania to London as a teenager, I included the more fashionable clothes I'd never had the confidence to wear in American schools, so I could transform myself into the "cool girl" I longed to be.

But as an adult on my first business trips, my attempts at being a confident, high-flying executive came crashing down, fast. For a final job interview, which required a flight from Seattle to Dallas, I forgot to pack shoes to wear for the meeting. Luckily, my sales skills came in handy, as I sweet-talked a manager into opening a department store early so I could purchase a pair of pointed black pumps before I caught my flight. That experience primed me for the long day of interviews, which resulted in an offer. It was a job I happily accepted.

It wasn't until my next job as a project manager that I learned the art of packing. I traveled for three weeks out of every month, and I visited the entire northeastern United States—western Massachusetts, northern New Jersey, Manhattan, and down to Virginia and Washington, D.C. I was in a constant state of packing, unpacking, and repacking. My job consumed so much of me that I had no time or energy for tackling the "what to wear and what to pack" internal debate.

Eventually, a handful of chic, classic clothing items emerged as my travel wardrobe. A pair of sharp flats and stylish yet modest heels have lived in my suitcase ever since, because I can coordinate them with everything else. Rather than swap out the jewelry each week, I put a mixture of colorful favorites into a classic leather clutch and tucked it alongside my travel toiletries. My suitcase shrank, my packing time decreased, and I became more confident in my role at work. I had figured out who I really wanted to be and how I could pack for achieving that.

I started running the meetings I used to simply record the notes for, negotiating the agreements I used to just hear reports about, and presenting the plans to potential partners

I used to know only by name. I entered the company as a project manager and left as the vice president of Business Development, having negotiated deals valued at over $300 million. It might sound like a stretch, but I attribute this success to learning how to pack perfectly.

Once I discovered the power of packing well, I wanted to help others to learn how to do it, too. I started a weekly online series on my blog, HithaOnTheGo.com, that focused on tips for addressing specific packing "pains." As the series grew in popularity, I began getting all kinds of personal, trip-specific questions from my readers, and so I started offering personalized packing sessions. I realized my clients had mental blocks about packing and there were common pitfalls.

In their everyday lives, these clients were generally confident, accomplished people. But as soon as the suitcase came out, they grew afraid, disorganized, and generally were all over the place, mentally and emotionally. They unraveled at the prospect of packing for a business trip, simply because that trip was so important; or they waited all year to visit a dream destination, only to be shivering the whole time because they hadn't brought warm enough clothing. By showing these clients that *how you pack is who you are,* I was able to help them become self-assured master packers. Their trips were better, and their family, friends, and colleagues enjoyed traveling with them so much more.

The method I outline in this book ensures that every one of your trips will reach its full potential, unhindered by inadequate packing. When you finish reading this book, you will have eliminated all those awful feelings we frequently associate with packing, like fear, anxiety, and insecurity, and you will have replaced them with self-assuredness and giddy anticipation of your next trip.

First, we'll identify your packing personality. When you understand the motivations behind *how* to pack, we'll dive into the nitty-gritty of creating a packing station at home, selecting the perfect travel clothing and accessories, and putting everything together, ready to be put to use at your destination. I'll have you racing through security and elevating your in-flight time.

It's time to pack perfect. Every trip, every time. Your journey starts here.

Find Your Packing Personality

Knowing where you need the most work is the first step toward becoming a more efficient traveler. We all have different "problem areas" when it comes to packing. You might identify strongly with one, two, or even all these types, but figuring out which characteristics describe you best will help you make good use of my method.

THE ANXIOUS OVERPACKER

- You fear not having something you think you might need.

- You think more is more.

- You need options, even if the options are all similar to one another.

- Your inclination is to take advantage of free checked bags when available.

- You spend mornings on your trip deciding what to wear and try on several things to see which looks best.

PACK PERFECT TIP: You need a confidence boost. You know what you need and you should feel empowered by ruthlessly editing your suitcase.

THE FOREVER FORGETFUL

- Your first stop upon landing is the nearest mall or drugstore to pick up what didn't make its way into your suitcase.

- You're often too hot or too cold because you didn't check the weather for your destination before packing.

- Your spouse has to double- and triple-check that you packed certain items, and friends and family call to remind you the night before a trip not to forget certain key items.

PACK PERFECT TIP: The packing checklist will be your strongest ally. Check it, double-check it, and then check it again. It will also help you stay focused on what you'll need.

THE JUMBLED TRAVELER

- Your clothes always come out of your luggage wrinkled.

- You've opened your bag to exploded shampoo.

- You toss items into your bag on your way out the door.

- You hold up the security line, piecing your belongings apart and back together.

- You spend a lot of time trying to locate items in the "black hole" of your in-flight bag.

PACK PERFECT TIP: Organizing your bags in a specific manner is important. Pay extra attention to the order items go in. Packing cubes and a folding board will be excellent tools.

THE IMPRACTICAL DAYDREAMER

- You're so excited about your upcoming trip that you don't think beyond long walks on the beach, forgetting that it gets chilly at night.

- You go out and buy a new, untested travel wardrobe because you believe you'll be a whole different person on this trip! You're on an adventure!

PACK PERFECT TIP: Realize your adventure is best served by good preparation. That means preparing to pack will actually add spontaneity. Power pieces will help ground you.

The Packing Timeline
How to Avoid "I'm Forgetting Something" Syndrome

When you pack at the last minute, you likely will lack confidence that you have packed everything you'll need. I had a client who always checked an enormous bag, thinking that if she brought lots of items, there would be a lower chance of forgetting something. What she ended up with was redundancies (think five black T-shirts), but without small essentials like hair ties. After she tried the packing timeline, she found she was packing in a fraction of the time and bringing a third of the stuff. We often fear the unknown, and we use the items we pack as "security" instead of employing our best organizational and planning skills. You spend months planning a trip, right? So, why are you packing the night before? This is when the packing timeline comes in handy. Let's take a look—and don't worry if you don't know what some of these things are yet. You will.

The week before...

7

Check your packing station. Decide which suitcase you're bringing and make sure it is in good condition, with a luggage tag. Are the wheels tight? Is the handle working? Keep the bag open and out for inspection.

Make sure your toiletry bag is stocked.

Load your travel wallet. Add your passport. Print any travel confirmations you'll need, as well as maps in the language of the country to which you are traveling, if appropriate. Print your itinerary.

Take a glance at your old photos from other trips and get excited!

6

Check the weather at your destination for a preliminary idea of what's ahead. Take out your blank packing list (more on that later) and start listing what your power pieces will be. Check to see that they're all clean; if not, dry-clean or launder them. This day covers the biggest bulk of packing: you should gain a general sense of what clothes you're bringing, so that you can choose your accessories tomorrow. For adventure trips, this includes gear.

5

DAYS BEFORE DEPARTURE

Pick out your accessories and shoes. Make sure everything is in good condition. Polish the shoes or drop them off at the cobbler. Clean out any extraneous things in your handbags.

4

DAYS BEFORE DEPARTURE

Pack your clothes using your packing list, checking off the items and editing as you go. Invite a friend or two over for consultation. Make a fun night of it with wine and cheese, and put on music. If they are going on the trip with you, even better, but it's not a requirement. Your friends will help you edit out what isn't necessary and give you the confidence that you are packing all the right things.

PACKING FOR TWO CLIMATES

If you're leaving a cold weather spot and going door to door to warm weather, you can make do with a pair of slip-on sneakers or flats instead of a bulky pair of boots. Be sure they're a style that can be worn with or without socks, so you can wear them again at your much warmer destination. Consider leaving and returning in a lightweight, packable down coat that folds into a tiny pouch (Uniqlo makes a great one). Use a cotton scarf instead of a wool one so it can double as a swimsuit cover-up at your destination. Try thin gloves and earmuffs for extra warmth without added bulk.

3
DAYS BEFORE DEPARTURE

Treat yourself to in-flight goodies, like a book or magazines and snacks.

2
DAYS BEFORE DEPARTURE

Using your checklist, pack your toiletries, shoes, and accessories. Get any pre-trip beauty treatments you're planning on—a manicure or pedicure, blowout, or wax appointment.

1
THE NIGHT BEFORE

Get a good night's sleep. Have a great dinner, hydrate, and set your alarm with confidence.

0
MORNING OF

Pack your in-flight bag using your in-flight checklist. Remember any last-minute essentials like makeup, medication, eyeglasses, electronics, and important jewelry, or anything precious you would never want to go missing.

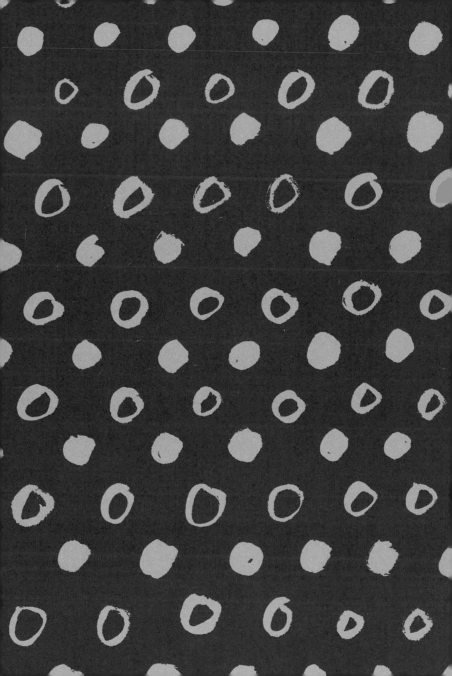

Preparing for Takeoff

HOW TO PRE-PACK

Anything worth achieving requires preparation. Suppose you want to bake a cake. You decide the kind of cake you want to make, gather the ingredients, lay them out on the counter, mix them together according to a recipe, and then enjoy the results in all their delicious glory. You prep for meetings, don't you? You wouldn't show up to an exam without preparing for it, so why not with packing? As with most other things in life, advance planning ensures the best outcome. This is called *pre-packing*.

Your basic ingredients are your suitcase and travel accessories. By establishing a packing station, you will be confident about the choices you make and will set a calm and organized tone for your trip. When you arrive at your destination, you'll know you have what you need, because you will have thoughtfully picked out every item in advance. You'll be setting yourself up to be at your best. Pre-packing is where your adventure begins. It's not when you step off the plane or out of the car; it's here, it's *now*. With planning.

A Carry-on Crash Course

When you're on the road, your suitcase is your home. That's why finding the right one for you is a key step to packing perfect. What's my rule? Don't buy a luggage set. You will end up with a fleet, the members of which you just might not need—and trust me when I tell you that you'll overspend. Instead, invest in your flagship piece: a carry-on suitcase that will meet all your needs. Let's discuss the details.

INTERNATIONAL CARRY-ON

These are the smallest of the carry-ons, usually standing at 21 inches or less. What they lack in space they make up for in convenience, as they meet nearly all airlines' carry-on size requirements, including those of local and regional budget airlines. By the time you're through this book, this intimidatingly small suitcase won't be so intimidating.

DOMESTIC CARRY-ON

Domestic carry-on suitcases are a little bit larger, ranging between 21 and 23 inches in height, with an extra inch of depth, too. These bags meet the requirements of most major U.S. and European airlines. If you're going to be hopping from city to city and flying smaller carriers or traveling by train or bus, you may have to check this suitcase at certain points.

HARD CASE

Hard cases are often lighter and easier to lift overhead than their soft-case counterparts, simply because of their material. If you choose a hard case, go with one that's constructed from polycarbonate. It can scratch easily, but it's very strong and can withstand rough handling.

SOFT CASE

While soft cases can be heavier because they are made with bulky, thick nylon, they are more durable and won't dent or scratch like their hard-case counterparts. If you know you'll be checking your bag on occasion, opt for a soft suitcase for its increased ruggedness. In that situation, the additional weight won't matter.

FOUR-WHEELER

All-direction four-wheeled models are convenient because you can drag your bag behind you and wheel it alongside you, as well as maneuver it around obstacles with ease.

TWO-WHEELER

While a two-wheeled bag can only be dragged behind you, it has the benefit of standing up securely without wheeling away on an incline. This model can also hold a heavier bag on top of it more securely than a four-wheeled case.

My flagship piece is a red, hard-case, four-wheeled international carry-on from Tumi. The color reminds me of red wine, and it is easy to spot in the overhead compartment. I went for the shorter model because carrying on my suitcase is always a high priority for me, and I wanted to make sure it met the requirements of every airline I might encounter. Quality is also important to me, so I have a lifetime warranty. When I know I'm checking a bag, I prefer a soft-case, two-wheeled suitcase because it's more stable and I'm rarely dragging it long distances.

Now it's time for you to decide which flagship pieces are right for you.

COLOR ME HAPPY

Your suitcase color is completely your preference. If you find a suitcase you love in a color that speaks to you, get it! Many folks recommend choosing one that is not black so you can spot it immediately, but if you prefer black or other neutral colors, then stick with that. Your suitcase is your home away from home, and you should love every element of it—especially the color. Personalize the suitcase with a monogram or a luggage tag in a beautiful print or bright color to make it all your own.

OTHER BAGS

A *weekender* or *duffel bag* is ideal for weekend trips or car trips, as you won't be carrying it for long periods of time and it can fit into the smallest of spaces (like the space under the seat in front of yours on a small plane). Look for a model that has a water-resistant lining and a separate shoe compartment; these features will help keep your belongings clean and organized.

A *backpack* is also a key addition to your luggage arsenal. Use it as your travel tote for camping or athletic trips, or when you need to be hands-free. It's also a great option for when you have quick connections or are traveling with kids.

A *garment bag* is ideal if you're packing formalwear or embellished items that are prone to excessive wrinkling. Make sure your garment bag has a shoulder strap (for easy carrying). Politely ask the flight attendants if they wouldn't mind hanging your bag in the plane's coat closet when you board.

I NEVER WANT MY SUITCASE TO BE CHECKED IN

I need to be able to lift my suitcase overhead by myself

I'd like to be able to wheel my suitcase alongside me

- International carry-on
- Hard case
- Four wheels

I'm fine with just dragging my suitcase behind me

- International carry-on
- Hard case
- Two wheels

I need my suitcase to be able to withstand external roughness

I'd like to be able to wheel my suitcase alongside me

- International carry-on
- Soft case
- Four wheels

I'm fine with just dragging my suitcase behind me

- International carry-on
- Soft case
- Two wheels

I DON'T MIND CHECKING IN MY SUITCASE OCCASIONALLY

I need to be able to lift my suitcase overhead by myself

I need my suitcase to be able to withstand external roughness

I'd like to be able to wheel my suitcase alongside me

I'm fine with just dragging my suitcase behind me

I'd like to be able to wheel my suitcase alongside me

I'm fine with just dragging my suitcase behind me

- Domestic carry-on
- Hard case
- Four wheels

- Domestic carry-on
- Hard case
- Two wheels

- Domestic carry-on
- Soft case
- Four wheels

- Domestic carry-on
- Soft case
- Two wheels

Items May Shift in Flight
Finding the Right Organizing Accessories

LARGER ITEMS

For the hyper-organized, packing accessories are a bonus. For the less well organized, they're a necessity. Having the right accessories saves you time, energy, and space. They do the work for you, and ultimately teach you how to pack. Get them in your favorite colors and bright, bold complementary prints. When you open your suitcase, they'll sparkle and make you feel happy. Here are the basic accessories.

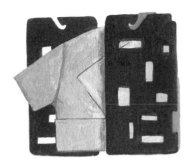

SHOE BAG

A light yet sturdy shoe bag will protect both your shoes and your clothes. Your bag should be able to fit three pairs of shoes. Choose one that is machine washable and made of durable canvas or nylon. While you can use a plastic shopping bag, the flimsy bag may rip easily and get your clothes dirty—which is the opposite of what you want! My favorite shoe bag is by Hudson+Bleecker—it's roomy enough to hold my shoes while fitting nicely inside my suitcase. Plus, they're available in fun, bold prints.

FOLDING BOARD

Folding boards can be your strongest organizational ally. Not only can you use them for packing, but they're great every time you do laundry. Using a folding board ensures that all your clothing is folded to the exact same size, which conserves space in the suitcase and helps min-imize wrinkles. You know how the stacks of T-shirts look in stores? There is something beautiful and satisfying about seeing your own clothes that way. It will help you decide how to edit your wardrobe for a trip, too.

PACKING CUBES

Packing cubes hold together your clothes within your suitcase. They also allow you to keep your clothing organized, help prevent wrinkles, and force you to pack compactly and efficiently. The packing cube should be durable and machine washable. Nothing out there will break the bank, but invest in something that will stand the test of time. Try to avoid mesh, since it tends to rip or snag—opt for nylon or canvas instead. I like the FLIGHT001 Spacepak, which holds all my clean rolled-and-folded clothes, and has a section for my dirty laundry. Test the zipper before your purchase; metal ones are best. Whether you choose to get a set of packing cubes or use only a single packing cube is up to you. But if you go with a set, make sure all of them fit on one side of your suitcase when they're filled up.

IN-FLIGHT BAG

I like to use a small nylon
tote bag that folds up small,
because it can double as a
great beach or laundry bag
in a pinch. And if I pick up
something on my trip that
I need to carry on the flight
as my second item, I can
use the tote bag to hold it as
well, and then put it overhead. If that item is bulky,
it will take up space at my
seat that would otherwise
be for legroom. My absolute
favorite is a foldable nylon
tote from Baggu.

TRAVEL STEAMER

Steam not only removes
the wrinkles from your
clothing but it also freshens
them, removing some odors.
Steaming is much easier
than ironing, and it works
on more types of fabrics and
garments, too. For some
of you, it might seem like
an over-the-top accessory,
but for me it's a basic. The
steamer I use is smaller and
lighter than a hairdryer,
so it doesn't take up much
space in my suitcase; the
fashionistas I know swear
by it. Plus, you can use its
chamber to pack other small
items that might otherwise
get lost.

TOILETRY BAG

Your toiletries should always be contained—this is where leaks and explosions tend to happen. And those can ruin a trip! So, always choose a bag with a water-resistant and easy-to-clean lining. A zippered, quart-size bag with a 2-inch width will carry all your liquid toiletries with ease. The width holds the items flat, avoiding any bulges that you might get with a plastic bag. You should keep this bag stocked with travel-size versions of everything you know you'll need. Medications and eyeglasses should be packed the day of your trip in your carry-on.

LAUNDRY BAG

As mentioned earlier, I prefer a packing cube that has a dirty-laundry compartment. But if you're keeping clean and dirty separate, bring along something durable made of thick canvas or nylon with a drawstring so you can separate your clothes. While you can certainly use the plastic bag provided by a hotel, the thin plastic doesn't trap odors as well as something stronger, and your whole suitcase could end up smelling like dirty socks. A more durable bag traps odors better. Plus, it's more environmentally friendly.

SMALLER ITEMS

JEWELRY CASE

What's worse than arriving at your destination with a tangle of chains? Your jewelry case should have a place to post earrings and multiple pockets to separate larger pieces from smaller, daintier ones. You should be able to hang long necklaces without any fear of their getting tangled. My Hudson+Bleecker jewelry case is as beautiful as the jewelry I pack inside it.

MAKEUP CASE

You should be packing any makeup in an easy-to-clean bag that's specifically designed for delicate items and brushes. For those more serious about cosmetics, a compartmentalized soft case with spaces for brushes and different zippered compartments also helps keep the products clean and organized. Stephanie Johnson makes a variety of makeup bags and brush cases to suit all needs.

CHARGER BAG

You don't need much more than a small pouch to hold your electronics chargers, but I highly recommend investing in duplicates of your most frequently used chargers and keeping them pre-packed in this pouch.

TRAVEL WALLET

Widely available, travel wallets are exceptionally helpful. They should have spaces for your passport, printouts of travel confirmations, frequent flyer cards, and a travel-friendly credit card.

Ground Control
Creating a Packing Station

Setting up a packing station in your home will make preparations for all your future trips more enjoyable and less harried. Designate a corner of your home just for travel and packing items. If you don't have the space to make it permanent, designate a shelf or two. In this spot you'll store your carry-on, in-flight bag, toiletry bag, and packing accessories, all together in the same place.

Add mementos and photos from past trips to put you in the right mindset from the get-go. Your packing station can be as dreamy as it is practical. Once you've created your station, you can start to imagine all the future trips you'll take. Feel the sun on your face, picture the beautiful architecture you'll see, the exotic food you'll eat, or the business trips at which you'll soar. You're well on your way to becoming a truly great traveler.

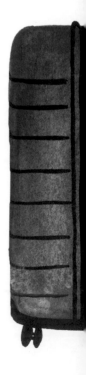

Ready to Wear

CHOOSING CLOTHES WITH STYLE

To most travelers, selecting the right clothing is the most daunting part of any packing experience. Don't psych yourself out; remember, you get dressed every day and look fantastic! We often think that packing those stylish outfits is somehow different from putting them together at home. It is not. On a daily basis, you gravitate to specific items that make you feel beautiful, powerful, and happy. The same applies to packing. When you go on a trip, you're still you—you're selecting clothing within the parameters of that place with which you're most familiar: your own closet! So let's talk about how to make the most of what you pack—and look good doing it.

Whatever the Weather

Weather is a key factor in deciding which pieces are necessary to pack. Most of us check the weather constantly before a trip, but it's still hard to know exactly what it will feel like when we're there. Sixty degrees can feel balmy or freezing, depending on your comfort level. When you check the forecast at your destination, consider factors like the evening temperature drop, the wind chill or humidity, and the precipitation forecast. If you know someone who lives there, certainly ask what he or she has been wearing most recently. Obviously, the temperature will inform everything that goes on your packing list.

Laying the Foundation
Barely There and Sleepwear

Undergarments are some of the most forgotten items. Or conversely, you may find it tough to figure out how much to pack, because everything seems so small—you figure you might just as well throw it all in! This approach adds up to packing way too much, and results in less space for the items you'll actually wear. Enter packing math. By following these simple equations, you'll have everything you need without being bogged down with extra bulk and superfluous options.

UNDERWEAR

NUMBER OF DAYS YOU'RE THERE **+** **HALF THE NUMBER OF DAYS YOU'RE THERE**

NOTE: If you bring white pants or a white dress, don't forget nude underwear!

BRAS

1 Black bra | 1 Strapless or convertible bra | 1 Nude bra

SHAPEWEAR

MATCH NUMBER TO SPECIFIC OUTFITS **+** **1 EXTRA BASIC AS BACKUP**

1 Set of sleepwear for every three days

+

1 Full loungewear outfit

Fit Fix
What to Pack for Working Out

When it comes to travel workout gear, select items that are made of quick-drying or wicking material. Not only are they more comfortable for your workouts, but they can also be washed and dried easily to wear again. Pack three workout outfits per week and wash your workout clothes in the sink after their first wearing. If possible, pack plain black leggings for your workout bottoms—they can do double duty for lounging around or when traveling back home.

Power Pieces That Earn a Spot

What is a *power piece*? Your power pieces are as original as you are, and they reflect your personal style. They're your go-to's. Some people feel that the old standbys or neutral power pieces are best for everyone, but they are not. We all have our own power pieces. Some of us always wear pants, while others love dresses. I personally feel most myself in classics: black cigarette pants, a sharp white blouse, a navy blazer. But I have a client who loves bright colors—and everything in her closet reflects her explosive personality. Her "neutrals" are Kelly green, marigold, and fuchsia. She would feel uncomfortable in my neutrals, and I in hers. The point is, you should feel at home when you are away and be at ease. What do you wear most frequently? What are you drawn to? What can you not live without? What features seamlessly flow through your whole wardrobe? Those are your power pieces. Maybe it's a chambray button-down or a chunky sweater jacket. Maybe it's a sturdy pencil skirt. Whatever your personal power pieces, here are some criteria for identifying them for travel.

BOTTOMS (SHORTS, PANTS, AND SKIRTS)

- You wear them more than any other bottom.

- They will not stretch after two wears.

- They are in your personal primary neutral color (usually navy, black, brown, or denim).

- They can accommodate any post-flight bloat or trip overindulgence.

- You don't need to look into your closet to think about them.

TOPS (BLOUSES AND SWEATERS)

- Their style complements the bottoms you're packing. My rule of thumb is a loose shirt for fitted bottoms and a fitted shirt for loose bottoms.

- They won't pill or shed on your clothing.

- They are in colors and prints that speak to you.

- They're not fussy or delicate.

- They look good on you 100 percent of the time.

DRESSES AND JUMPSUITS

- They are appropriate and respectful for where they're being worn. Examine the neckline, hemline, and how tightly the dress fits to make sure it suits the setting.

- They are always flattering. Traveling can add a pound or two to your frame. Pick dresses that make you look your best even on your worst days.

OUTERWEAR

- It meets the low end of the weather forecast (including wind chill or humidity) and any inclement weather predicted.

- It complements the other clothing you've selected.

How to Get the Most from Every Power Piece

Now that you know what your power pieces are, you can start using them to the full extent of their, well, power. This is where you begin the mental shift toward becoming a power packer. Instead of thinking about your clothes in terms of single outfits, reimagine your suitcase as a compact bundle of HUIs (High Usage Items). That means mixing and matching. Laying out complete outfits—as most do—is the number one cause of overpacking. If you're thinking of separate outfits, you're automatically packing more pieces than you actually need, because you're most likely not going to wear them more than once.

As you mentally catalogue your power pieces, imagine how you would wear them as many times as the chart on page 45 suggests. Don't freak out, though. Consider how you usually wear them; traveling doesn't have to change that. The numbers of wears suggested in the chart are just that— suggestions. If you can't think of five ways to wear a blazer, does that mean it can't come with you? Not necessarily. These are goals, and it obviously depends on the itinerary of your trip. But the bottom line is this: the bulk of the clothing in your suitcase should be highly wearable and hardworking. (When we get to the sample packing lists on pages 73–83, you'll see examples of power pieces at work and how many different ways they can be worn on a single trip. *That's* how you pack perfect.)

T-shirts

2 wears (SEE TIP ON PG. 47)

Blouses

2–3 wears

Sweaters

3–4 wears

Blazer

4–5 wears

Bottoms

2–3 wears

Dress

2–3 wears

Fantasy Pieces
Choosing Silk or Sequins

I'm all about fantasy. I love the idea of meeting a handsome stranger on a trip and living happily ever after. That's actually how I met my husband! In my fantasy, I'm wearing an embellished cocktail dress and stunning high heels, dancing the night away at a sparkling affair. In reality, I was wearing a bright yellow skirt paired with a black cardigan and sensible black ballet flats. In packing, you strike a balance.

Even though you're still you when you're away from home, sometimes you are a "getaway" you—the best you. There's nothing wrong with daydreaming about how beautiful you'll look in a flowery dress, sipping Champagne in a little French garden, but the reality is that you'll likely be making a long trek down the allée of a garden to get there, and the temperature will drop before you are back at your hotel. You

LOOK LIKE A LOCAL

There's a delicate balance between looking like your best self and fitting in with the locals. While head-to-toe black works perfectly in New York City, it's out of place in Charleston or Miami. If looking like a local is important to you, do a little research. A quick social media search of "fashion" + the city of your destination will pull up tons of images of what the locals are wearing. While you shouldn't go out and buy a brand-new wardrobe for that southern trip, you may want to swap a plain top for a floral one or that second pair of dark pants for a breezy skirt.

might also need a perfectly fitted trench coat so you don't have to buy a touristy sweatshirt or ill-fitting sweater—if you ignore reality, the fantasy gets ruined.

I don't want to squash the fantasy though; these pieces do have a place. Single-occasion dresses are ideal because they take up the least amount of space. They're typically associated with a big event like a wedding or gala, at which you would wear your planned outfit just once, even if you were home. So, once you've referred to the dress code, let your style imagination run wild. Remember: fantasy pieces are not only reserved for dressy occasions; for nearly any trip, you can pack a piece that you absolutely *love*—a sequined blazer to wear to dinner one night, cool leather pants, or that lace-trimmed dress that makes you feel like a million dollars. Just limit your fantasy item to one per five-day trip, and no more than three fantasy pieces maximum—ever.

T-SHIRT TIME

When it comes to tops, T-shirt power pieces have different qualities from blouses or sweaters. While white T-shirts are a classic, they show dirt and stain more easily than gray or dark T-shirts, so opt for the latter when traveling. They are often a wear-once item, but can and should be repurposed for working out or sleeping in before they hit the laundry bag.

Airing Your Dirty Laundry
How to Keep Your Clothes Clean on the Go

The underlying problem in any successful outfit remix is how to keep your clothes clean without succumbing to the overpriced laundry service at a hotel. Believe it or not, you already have everything you need to refresh your stuff while you're away. Take a few extra minutes at

Clothing Type	What You'll Need
Underwear and workout clothes	Hotel room shampoo
Light fabric items (cotton, silk, denim)	Fabric refresher spray such as Febreze or a steamer and essential oils
Heavy items (wools, knits)	Dryer sheets

the end of each day of your trip to quickly spruce up anything you plan to re-wear. The following table offers some tips on cleaning your travel clothing.

How to Clean It
Plug the drain and fill the sink with hot water and a quarter-size dollop of shampoo.
Place 2–3 items in the sink and massage them with the soapy water.
Drain the sink and rinse each item thoroughly.
Hang the items on the towel or shower curtain rod to dry.
With the spray, spritz each garment at an 8-inch distance. Hang to release wrinkles and dry.
With the steamer, add 1–2 drops essential oil to the steamer chamber and fill with water. Plug it in. Once the steam starts coming out, carefully steam the wrinkles out of your clothes. Hang to dry.
Lay the garment on the bed and rub a dryer sheet all over the item. Turn over, and repeat. Hang the item with a dryer sheet placed inside the garment for additional freshening.

Transit Chic
What to Wear When You Travel

Travel outfits have to walk a fine line between stylish and comfortable. You'll want to select items suited for a long day of travel, but that can also be worn during your trip and your return journey home. Lightweight layers will keep you cozy and chic at the same time.

1. Ponte leggings or stretchy jeans will allow for maximum comfort.

2. A cotton tank breathes and provides an additional layer or extra warmth.

3. A long-sleeved T-shirt is just the right weight, whether your flight is chilly or warm.

4. A blazer or cardigan will keep you warm and add extra polish to your outfit while doubling as a great outerwear piece when arriving at your destination.

5. A large scarf can be used as a fashion piece or an in-flight blanket.

6. Compression or cashmere socks keep you warm and are better than bare feet while going through security.

Now that you have an understanding of power pieces versus fantasy pieces, what to wear in flight, and how to take care of it all on the go, you will be able to best select and edit clothing for your trip. You might have thought packing was just about putting things into your suitcase and maybe how to roll or fold certain items (and we'll get to that), but now that you're able to cover all your clothing bases, from pajamas to cocktail dresses, you're well on your way to becoming a pro-packer.

5.

3.

2.

6.

1.

4.

HINT: Pack a clean T-shirt and underwear in your in-flight bag if you're taking an overnight flight. After a long trip, these changes will help you feel fresh. Also pack a Baggie for your dirty ones!

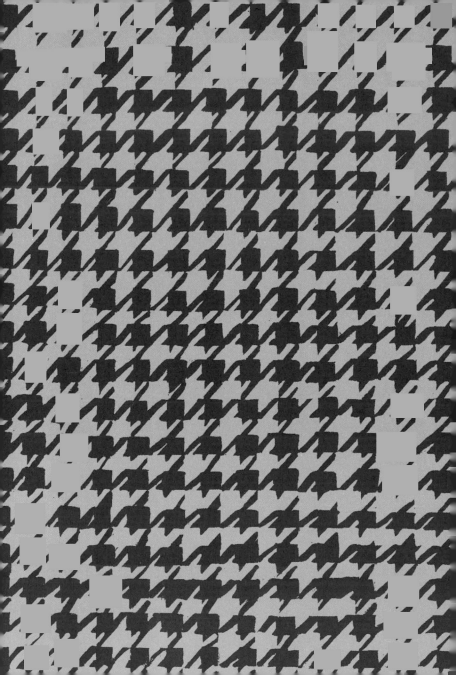

Secret Weapons

Your accessories are the details that make you feel polished. They render your look unique and keep you rooted in your own skin when you're dressing with a limited wardrobe. You don't want to lack substance in this area simply because you're away—nor do you need to. Let's talk about how to pack perfect when it comes to these small yet powerful items.

The Accessory Math Secret
Adding Up to Your Best Look

You should select your accessories the way you choose a candle to light or a book to read. That is, you can only ever use one of each type at a time, and you instinctively know which to reach for, depending on your mood. The same goes for accessories. You're only wearing one pair of shoes or carrying one bag at a single time, so choose your accessories wisely. Power pieces aren't just for clothing; the rules apply here, too.

Imagine all your favorite accessories. Now edit them by applying the accessory math.

This equation is of utmost importance. If you only follow one piece of advice in this book, this is it. Following this rule will drastically change the way you pack. Everyone over-packs accessories, thinking they are small. Stick to the math!

THREE PAIRS OF SHOES

TWO BAGS

Scarf   **ONE OF EACH**   Sunglasses

Hat
(Optional)

Belt
(Optional)

Let's break it down a little further. Just as with clothing, you should strike a balance between accessory power pieces and fantasy pieces. Two pairs of your shoes, your large bag, and your sunglasses should always be your power pieces. If you work out regularly, one of these power pairs of shoes will be your sneakers. If it's important to you to have a second pair of stylish flats or heels, consider doing workouts that don't require sneakers on your trip, whether it's a yoga sequence in your hotel room or a spin class where you can rent shoes. One pair of shoes and your small bag can be your fantasy pieces, particularly if you have a fantasy outfit for a special occasion. Your scarf is somewhere in the middle; it should be suited to the climate of your destination and how you plan to wear it, but you can have fun with the color or print! The same goes for the hat, though it and the belt are optional. You can pack as much jewelry as you like, as long as it fits easily in a single case, pouch, or small bag.

Coupling Up
Grouping Items the Right Way

This is when those wonderful packing tools you bought come in handy. Use them now to group your accessories and you will stay organized.

Use the various compartments and features of your case to pack your jewelry perfectly. Pierce your earrings through mini holes and use zippered sections to pack small necklaces and bracelets.

Your two smallest pairs of shoes go into the shoe bag. You will be wearing the bulkiest ones! Pack your pumps toe-to-heel, and pack socks and tights in the small spaces left by the shoes.

Stuff your scarf or other small items in the cap of your hat, and place it brim side down in your suitcase. Pack heavier items, like clothes or accessories, on top of the hat to help keep its shape.

Loop your belt inside the collar of a crisp blouse to keep it from being crushed.

Now you can see clearly how easy it is to fall into the "pile on" mode when it comes to accessories. If you're already a minimalist in this area, that's great; but even if you are of the "more is more" category, you can fall back on Accessory Math to keep things under control and still look great.

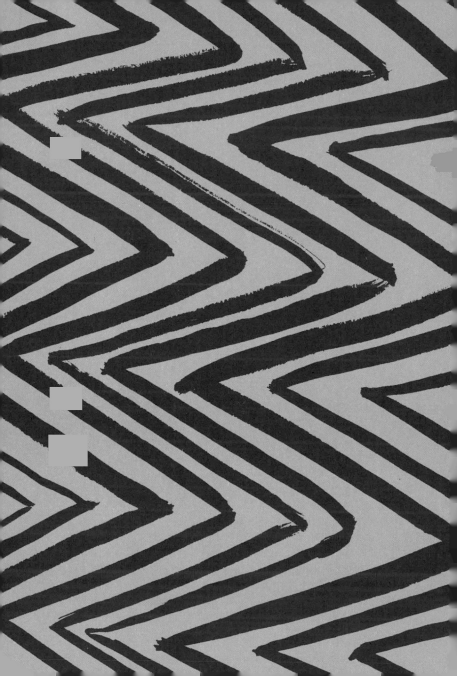

Pack Pretty

TOILETRY NEEDS AND BEAUTY MUST-HAVES

Traveling is no reason not to look your brightest and most beautiful. Whether it's the moisturizer that makes your skin feel perfect, your trusty mascara, or the only hair product that can tame your wild mane, you want to feel your best on every trip. That's where the science of the pared-down, miniature versions of your generally massive bottles of lotions and potions come into play. This chapter includes how to pack everything from the essentials in your at-home pharmacy to your favorite lip gloss.

From the Loo
All the Toiletries You'll Ever Need

Let's start with your toiletries. A quick inventory of your daily toiletries will help you figure out what you will need and how to pack those items efficiently. First things first: examine your medicine cabinet and note what you use the most regularly—twice a day, once a day, and every few days. Do it now—record them on this form.

Once you've filled out the form, take a moment and mark the ones that are must-pack, nonnegotiable products. If your hair is very particular and only responds to a specific routine and products, list that. If you're open to using any kind of body wash, leave that off the list.

Most important, separate your liquids and non-liquids. Liquid toiletries are constrained to only enough containers of 3 fluid ounces each to fill a quart-size bag, but you can pack full-size solids and powders in a much larger bag.

Let's look at the liquids. The listed toiletries—your must-haves and can't-live-withouts—are ones you should purchase in travel-size versions or decant into 3-fluid-ounce tubes or bottles. Examine the remainder of liquid items on your list, and see what you can eliminate—either by using the hotel-provided versions (like body lotion) or by substituting a towelette or solid version (think facial cleansing cloths). Do a little research and experiment before you finalize your swaps, then purchase and add them to your liquids bag.

TWICE DAILY	
Liquid	*Non-Liquid*

ONCE DAILY	
Liquid	*Non-Liquid*

ON OCCASION	
Liquid	*Non-Liquid*

Beauty junkies, this is a great time to shine: Birchbox offers travel-size samples for just this situation. Even if you're not signed up for their monthly beauty samples, look for samples of your favorite items in department stores, pharmacies, and even online. Next time you're at the hair salon, see if they have that styling balm in mini size!

For toiletries you may need only once or a small amount of, use a clean contact lens case to pack and store them. For example, I pack a single serving of shampoo and conditioner in a lens case. This trick works great for eye cream, lip scrub, cuticle oil, and the like, as well.

The zippered quart-size bag mentioned on page 32 is essential for maximizing the number of liquid products you can pack. It holds more products than a flat plastic zippered bag, and will last you countless trips. Pack the rigid 3-fluid-ounce containers first—your jars and tubs; then squeeze your most flexible and smallest containers in the spaces left. Last to go in the bag are your smallest containers and contact lens cases filled with liquids.

TRY COCONUT OIL

Coconut oil is a powerhouse toiletry, as it can be used for your teeth, face, and body. It can remove stubborn makeup, tame wayward eyebrows, act as shave gel and as cuticle cream, be a mouthwash that doubles as a teeth whitener, and save you from a nasty hangover. A full 3-fluid-ounce tube of coconut oil is worth the real estate in your liquids bag.

While travelers are restricted to a mere 3 fluid ounces (6 tablespoons) of each liquid toiletry, there are no such limits for non-liquid products. And just as you have for your liquid products, it's best to invest in a durable (and beautiful!) bag for your non-liquid products. If you're a beauty minimalist, a Dopp kit may be right for you. A Dopp kit is a small, zippered pouch with a rounded top and a flat bottom. Your other option is a double-handled, zippered toiletry case that offers much more space (but also occupies more space in your suitcase). Before you go out and purchase these bags, though, spread out all your non-liquids and examine them. Will they all fit into a small bag, or will you need more room or the ability to organize them by type? Pick the bag that works the best for you and your products, and keep it pre-packed and in your packing station. Load it up in the same way as the liquids: rigid and bulky at the bottom, flexible and small at the top. At the end of your trip, do a quick audit and replace any empty products with full ones.

Globetrotter Gorgeous
How to Edit Your Beauty Routine (and Still Look Great)

Traveling is a time to look like the healthy, vibrant, and happy person you are. Here's how to pack makeup the smart way.

- Make sure you have enough of everything you'll need ahead of time. You don't want to run out right before you leave, or worse, have to find it while you're away.

- Invest in multiples. Products with dual purposes, such as a lip/cheek duo, tinted moisturizer, or foundation with SPF save space.

- Opt for pencils over pots, which require a brush for application (e.g., eyeliner).

- Illuminator sticks and a bright lip color can wake up dull skin with little effort. A few swishes and dabs, and you'll look refreshed.

- If you use department-store products, ask for samples to use as travel-size cosmetics.

- Get trip-specific. For example, omit the glittery eye shadow if you're going on a business trip—you probably won't need it.

- Call ahead. Most hotels have blow dryers, so you can leave yours at home. Pack only one hair tool.

- If your hair requires multiple products, make swaps with other nonessential liquid toiletries to conserve space.

- Have bobby pins and hair ties for on-the-go updos.

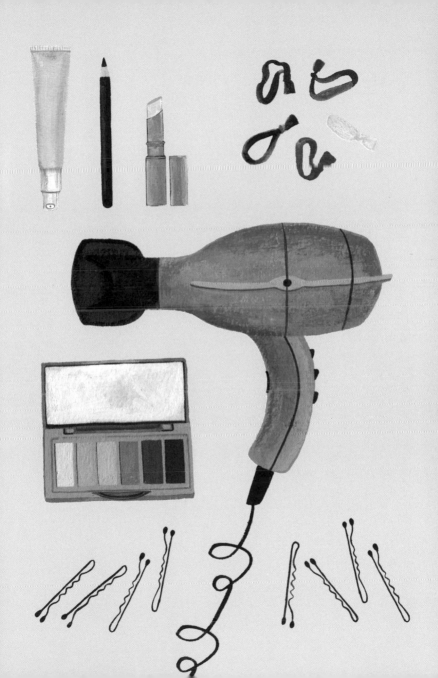

The key to packing light in the toiletry department is not to worry too much about running out of something. You always need less than you think! If you're afraid of not having enough of something, look into getting it in a non-liquid form, since you can pack that in larger quantities. For instance, dry shampoo powder will give you another day without a need for shampoo, and face wash can be supplemented with towelettes. The most satisfying part of implementing the tips in this chapter will be seeing all your toiletry and beauty needs packed in a concise and compartmentalized way.

TIP: How do you pack your makeup without forgetting any of it? You put it into your bag in the order of how you apply it—either as you get ready that morning or mimicking the process the night before, if you aren't wearing makeup to travel.

IN-FLIGHT SPA

Arriving at your destination fresh faced is easier than you think—and you'll always feel great when you step off a plane in style. The key is hydration. A common mistake is wearing too much powder, thinking that a full face of makeup will leave you looking just as good when you land as when you boarded. Instead, if you can, go to the airport bare-faced and then give yourself a hydrating facial in-flight. Here's how:

- Dab a thick balm on your cuticles and elbows.

- Apply hand cream.

- Apply a rich eye cream or coconut oil around your eyes.

- Apply a facial sheet mask before going to sleep. You may look funny to the other passengers, but you'll be the one with glowing skin upon arrival. Look for a product with hyaluronic acid or collagen.

- Clean off the mask with a cleansing towelette, and apply an emollient face cream.

- Before landing, refresh your face with another towelette or facial spray.

- Just before landing, apply concealer and tinted moisturizer, fill in your eyebrows, and use that multiple lip and cheek color you picked up (page 66). You'll walk off the plane as the most radiant version of yourself.

THE
PERFECT
PACKING
LISTS

We're almost on our way. These sample packing lists are my trade secrets. They are guides to beginning a process that will ultimately yield a beautifully arranged suitcase. My streamlined method will be challenging at first (don't necessarily expect to pack this lightly the first time you try), but push yourself to edit as much as possible. As you get more and more confident in your packing skills, you will find the process incredibly satisfying. Once you start filling out these lists for yourself, you're already on your way to being a pro-packer.

After you've identified your power pieces and selected your accessories, it's time to start making them work for you. Remember from page 44 that you are aiming for maximum wear first and outfit assembly second. On the pages that follow are sample packing lists for common types of trips. You'll see that by planning each day, you get the most out of every item that has earned a spot in your suitcase. You will find blanks in the back of this book, or on my website at HithaOnTheGo.com. Tear them out, tuck them in your suitcase, and store them in your packing station for the next trip.

BUSINESS TRIP

Destination: Chicago, IL

Length of Trip: 5 days

Weather Report: 52–68°F, sunny

OUTFITS

Day 1	Day 2	Day 3	Day 4	Day 5
AM	AM	AM	AM	AM
Black pants	Navy dress	Black skirt	Navy dress	Black pants
White blouse		White blouse	Navy blazer	Tan sweater
Navy blazer		Tan sweater		
PM	PM	PM	PM	PM
Black pants	Navy dress	Black skirt	Navy dress	Black pants
White blouse		White blouse	Navy blazer	Tan sweater
Navy blazer		Tan sweater		

CLOTHING

Tops	Bottoms	Dresses
1. White blouse	1. Black pants	1. Navy dress
2. Tan sweater	2. Black skirt	2.
3. Navy blazer	3.	3.
4.	4.	4.
5.	5.	5.

Underwear	Pajamas/Lounge	Workout
8 underpants	1 pajamas	2 workout pants
3 bras	1 lounge outfit	4 workout tops
5 socks	1 robe	4 sports bras
shapewear: Spanx slip		

SHOES

Black pumps	Navy flats	Sneakers

BAGS

Gray tote	Black cross-body bag

OTHER ACCESSORIES

[X] Sunglasses	[X] Scarf	[ ] Hat
[X] Belt	[X] Jewelry	

TOILETRIES

[X] Liquids	[X] Non-Liquids	[X] Beauty

ELECTRONICS

[X] Laptop	[ ] Tablet	[X] Phone
[X] Charger	[ ] Charger	[X] Charger
[ ] Headphones		

There's more to dressing for the job than you may realize. Know your audience, consider the industry, and bear in mind the purpose of your trip. If you feel confident you can get away with a bright color or high heels, then go for it.

Of course, don't forget any necessary papers or electronic devices. You'll never regret packing extra business cards. Have a vent clip and a car charger on hand for navigating a new city in your rental car. And remember, the most important accessory to bring on a business trip is confidence!

WEDDING WEEKEND

Destination: Nantucket, MA

Length of Trip: 3 days

Weather Report: 61–72°F

OUTFITS

Day 1	Day 2	Day 3
AM	AM	AM
White T-shirt	White button-down	Gray T-shirt
Skinny jeans		Skinny jeans
Cardigan		Cardigan
PM	PM	PM
Colored cocktail dress	Colored silk dress	Gray T-shirt
	Cashmere wrap	Skinny jeans
		Cardigan

CLOTHING

Tops	Bottoms	Dresses
1. White T-shirt	1. Skinny jeans	1. Cocktail dress
2. Gray T-shirt	2.	2. Silk dress
3. White button-down	3.	3.
4. Purple cardigan	4.	4.
5.	5.	5.

Underwear	Pajamas/Lounge	Workout
5 underpants	1 pajamas	1 workout pants
3 bras	1 lounge outfit	1 workout tops
0 socks	1 robe	1 sports bras
shapewear: Spanx slip		

SHOES

Gold strappy heels	Converse sneakers	Black flip-flops

BAGS

Tan leather tote	Gold clutch

OTHER ACCESSORIES

[X] Sunglasses	[X] Scarf	[ ] Hat
[X] Belt	[X] Jewelry	

TOILETRIES

[X] Liquids	[X] Non-Liquids	[X] Beauty

ELECTRONICS

[ ] Laptop	[ ] Tablet	[X] Phone
[ ] Charger	[ ] Charger	[X] Charger
[X] Headphones		

Wedding weekends are all about your look at the formal events. What you'll be wearing in between is often casual and much less important. After identifying your fantasy pieces for those main events, choose the right shapewear. Try everything on before you pack it! Does it need a trip to the tailor? You might want to bring a few more makeup products and hair accessories if you're doing your hair and makeup yourself. Don't forget jewelry—put it in a hotel safe immediately upon arrival, and be sure not to forget it when you check out. Remember that different types of weddings have different customs, so be sure to ask the bride and groom if you're expected to wear (or not wear) a certain color, cover your head, or cover your shoulders. Don't forget a gift for the bride and groom—and a smile!

CITY TRIP

Destination: San Francisco, CA

Length of Trip: 5 days

Weather Report: 54–75°F

OUTFITS

Day 1	Day 2	Day 3	Day 4	Day 5
AM	AM	AM	AM	AM
Black jeans	Skinny jeans	Black jeans	Cotton black dress	Blue jeans
Gray T-shirt	Plaid button-down	Chambray top	Chambray top	Printed button-down
Black blazer				Black blazer
PM	PM	PM	PM	PM
Black jeans	Cotton black dress	Black jeans	Cotton black dress	
White silk tank		White silk tank		
Black blazer		Black blazer		

CLOTHING

Tops	Bottoms	Dresses
1. Gray T-shirt	1. Black jeans	1. Cotton black dress
2. Printed button-down	2. Skinny jeans	2.
3. White silk tank	3.	3.
4. Chambray top	4.	4.
5. Black blazer	5.	5.

Underwear	Pajamas/Lounge	Workout
8 underpants	1 pajamas	3 workout pants
3 bras	1 lounge outfit	5 workout tops
8 socks	1 robe	5 sports bras
shapewear: Spanx slip		

SHOES

Black sneakers	Tan loafers	Floral heels

BAGS

Camel tote	Red leather cross-body bag

OTHER ACCESSORIES

[x] Sunglasses	[ ] Scarf	[x] Hat
[x] Belt	[x] Jewelry	

TOILETRIES

[x] Liquids	[x] Non-Liquids	[x] Beauty

ELECTRONICS

[x] Laptop	[x] Tablet	[x] Phone
[x] Charger	[x] Charger	[x] Charger
[x] Headphones		

My favorite vacations are to other cities. There is no better way to get to know another culture than getting lost in a new city, popping in and out of cafés and restaurants, and peering through the windows of little boutiques. Test your walking shoes before you leave to make sure they don't give you blisters and are comfortable for long periods of time. And learn to love layering! If you're walking around in warmer weather all day and then going straight into a chillier evening, you'll want to pack breathable layers to stay comfortable.

BEACH/LAKE VACATION

Destination: Barbados

Length of Trip: 5 days

Weather Report: 70–87°F

OUTFITS

Day 1	Day 2	Day 3	Day 4	Day 5
AM	AM	AM	AM	AM
Linen pants	Black bikini	White one-piece	Black bikini	Linen pants
White tank	Striped caftan	Cover-up	Floral dress	White T-shirt
Cover-up		Denim shorts		Cover-up
PM	PM	PM	PM	PM
Solid maxi dress	Linen pants	Floral dress	Maxi dress	
	Black silk tank			

CLOTHING

Tops	Bottoms	Dresses
1. White cotton tank	1. Linen pants	1. Maxi dress
2. Black silk tank	2. Denim shorts	2. Floral dress
3. Printed cover-up	3.	3.
4. Striped caftan	4.	4.
5. White T-shirt	5.	5.

Underwear	Pajamas/Lounge	Workout
__8__ underpants	__1__ pajamas	__2__ workout pants
__3__ bras	__1__ lounge outfit	__4__ workout tops
__8__ socks	__1__ robe	__4__ sports bras
shapewear: Spanx slip		

SHOES

Tan flip-flops	Gold heeled sandals	Sneakers

BAGS

Camel tote	Red leather bucket bag

OTHER ACCESSORIES

[X] Sunglasses	[ ] Scarf	[X] Hat
[ ] Belt	[X] Jewelry	

TOILETRIES

[X] Liquids	[X] Non-Liquids	[X] Beauty

ELECTRONICS

[ ] Laptop	[X] Tablet	[X] Phone
[ ] Charger	[X] Charger	[X] Charger
[X] Headphones		

Sitting on a beach is the best way to unwind. Make sure you have a great beach hat and lots of SPF. A bad burn can ruin a trip you've been looking forward to for months. Of course, multiple suits and chic cover-ups are key, as well as a pair of sunglasses powerful enough to shield your eyes from the tropical sun. The clothes you'll be wearing here are light, so packing light should be a (literal) breeze.

BUSINESS/CITY WEEKEND TRIP

Destination: Portland, OR

Length of Trip: 5 days

Weather Report: 48–61°F

OUTFITS

Day 1	Day 2	Day 3	Day 4	Day 5
AM	AM	AM	AM	AM
Black pants	Navy dress	Black dress	Blue jeans	Blue jeans
White blouse		Gray blazer	Tan sweater	Gray T-shirt
Gray blazer				Gray blazer
PM	PM	PM	PM	PM
Black pants	Navy dress	Black dress	Blue jeans	
White blouse		Cashmere wrap	White blouse	
Gray blazer				

CLOTHING

Tops	Bottoms	Dresses
1. White blouse	1. Black jeans	1. Navy dress
2. Tan sweater	2. Blue jeans	2. Black dress
3. Gray blazer	3.	3.
4. Gray T-shirt	4.	4.
5. Chambray top	5.	5.

Underwear	Pajamas/Lounge	Workout
__8__ underpants	__1__ pajamas	__2__ workout pants
__3__ bras	__1__ lounge outfit	__4__ workout tops
__5__ socks	__1__ robe	__4__ sports bras
shapewear: Spanx slip		

SHOES

Black pumps	Navy flats	Sneakers

BAGS

Gray tote	Black cross-body bag

OTHER ACCESSORIES

- [x] Sunglasses
- [x] Scarf
- [ ] Hat
- [x] Belt
- [x] Jewelry

TOILETRIES

- [x] Liquids
- [x] Non-Liquids
- [x] Beauty

ELECTRONICS

- [x] Laptop
- [ ] Tablet
- [x] Phone
- [x] Charger
- [ ] Charger
- [x] Charger
- [x] Headphones

Feel free to combine two of these lists—a destination wedding and a beach vacation, a business trip extended to a city weekend, and so on. However, my tip is that you try to separate your suitcase by trip segment. For instance, if you're transitioning from a business trip to a beach vacation, put your work attire in one pouch and your beach clothes in another. That will allow you to easily navigate your suitcase throughout the trip. Don't get flummoxed by the fact that you're combining trips and use it as an excuse to overpack. Remember, bringing minimal items equals maximum enjoyment! This is a situation to fold jackets and roll casual clothes as neatly as possible.

LONG TRIP

Destination: NYC/Philly/DC

Length of Trip: 10 days

Weather Report: 52—71°F

OUTFITS

Day 1	Day 2	Day 3	Day 4	Day 5
AM	AM	AM	AM	AM
Black leggings	Blue jeans	Black jeans	Blue jeans	Black jeans
Tan sweater	White T-shirt	Chambray top	Tan sweater	Gray T-shirt
	Black trench			
PM	PM	PM	PM	PM
Denim dress	Blue jeans	Chambray top		Black jeans
	Floral blouse	Gray skirt		Floral top

Day 6	Day 7	Day 8	Day 9	Day 10
AM	AM	AM	AM	AM
Black leggings	Denim dress	Black jeans	Black T-shirt	Blue jeans
Black T-shirt		Floral blouse	Black trench	Tan sweater
Black trench				
PM	PM	PM	PM	PM
	Denim dress	Black jeans	Black dress	
		Floral blouse	Tan scarf	

SHOES

Converse sneakers	Black pumps	Black ankle boots

BAGS

Black leather tote	Cobalt blue satchel

CLOTHING

Tops	Bottoms	Dresses
1. White T-shirt	1. Black leggings	1. Denim shirtdress
2. Gray T-shirt	2. Blue skinny jeans	2. Black T-shirt dress
3. Black T-shirt	3. Black skinny jeans	3.
4. Chambray top	4. Gray jersey skirt	4.
5. Floral blouse	5.	5.
6. Tan sweater	6.	6.
7. Black trench	7.	7.

Underwear	Pajamas/Lounge	Workout
15 underpants	3 pajamas	5 workout pants
5 bras	2 lounge outfit	8 workout tops
12 socks	1 robe	8 sports bras
shapewear: N/A		

Any trip that's 10 days or longer is a *long* trip. You'll find your suitcase is filled just a little bit more, and you'll wonder if a checked bag would be a better option. You can still fit everything into a carry-on—just pay special attention to keeping the items that come with you clean and rewearable. If you're renting an apartment, the unit might even have a washer/dryer.

When figuring out what to pack for a long trip, still refer to the specific trip-type list for item suggestions. Accessories, toiletries, and electronics follow the same guidelines as any other packing list.

Putting It All Together

HOW TO PACK FOR MAXIMUM SPACE

A perfectly packed suitcase is satisfying to zip closed before takeoff, and it feels like a breath of fresh air when unzipped upon arrival at your hotel. This chapter explains the benefits of rolling and folding, and how to pack everything for maximum space with minimum effort. Like anything else, it might be a bit challenging at first, but once you see the benefits of compact packing and easy use while you're on vacation, you'll never look back. After a few times, it will become second nature and you'll be doing it forever.

Folding vs. Rolling

There are two camps in the battle of clothes packing: the folders and the rollers. Both certainly can tout the advantages of either method. In the case of folding, it's faster to do, and many of your items are already folded at home. But rolling takes up less space overall, and it has the added benefit of reducing potential wrinkles. How's a traveler to know which team to join?

The best-packed suitcases contain a combination of folded and rolled clothing—sometimes, both in the same article of clothing!

How to Fold

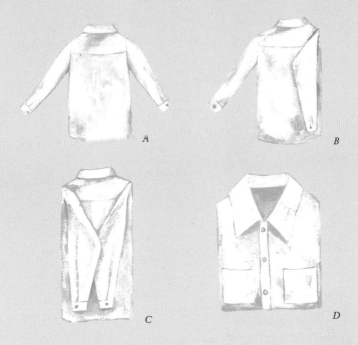

A

B

C

D

1. Lay article of clothing on a flat surface, with the front facing down. *(FIG. A)*

2. Fold in one sleeve and one-fourth of the shirt. *(FIG. B)*

3. Repeat on the other side. *(FIG. C)*

4. Fold the bottom of the shirt to the top, and flip over so the front is facing upward. *(FIG. D)*

BEST FOR: items made of delicate material (think silk, cashmere, and embellished pieces). Fold them in tissue paper to protect against damage from other items in your suitcase. Collars should always be facing upward and packed at the top of your bag to prevent crushing. Stuff small items (undergarments, socks, scarves) inside the collars to preserve their shapes.

How to Roll

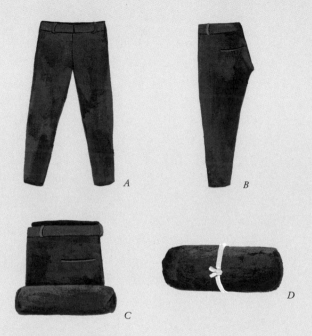

1. Lay article of clothing on
   a flat surface, bottom flat,
   front side facing up. *(FIG. A)*

2. Fold in half (along the seam,
   if applicable). *(FIG. B)*

3. Begin rolling the item from
   the short side. *(FIG. C)*

4. Arrange in the suitcase
   with the roll opening down.
   (FIG. D)

BEST FOR: All bottoms (pants, shorts, skirts), dresses, jackets, and non-collared tops. Secure items with hair ties to keep them rolled up in transit.

How to Combo Fold/Roll

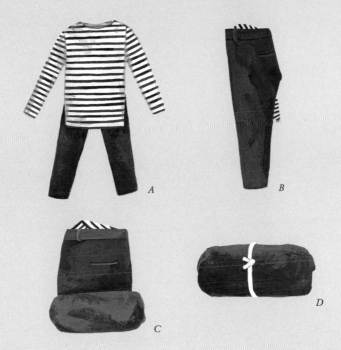

1. Lay articles of clothing on top of each other, with the longest item at the bottom. *(FIG. A)*

2. Fold all the items in half lengthwise. *(FIG. B)*

3. Roll the items tightly. *(FIG. C)*

4. Secure the outfit roll with a hair tie. *(FIG. D)*

How to Pack Jackets

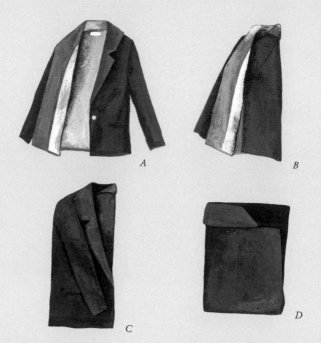

A

B

C

D

1. Lay jacket on a flat surface with the front facing upward. *(FIG. A)*

2. Open one side of the jacket at the armhole.

3. Pull the opposite sleeve through the open side. *(FIG. B)*

4. Fold the opening closed, and both sleeves across the jacket. *(FIG. C)*

5. Roll the jacket, starting from the bottom all the way up to the collar. *(FIG. D)*

BEST FOR: Blazers, trench coats, and lightweight jackets.

What Goes in First
The Art of the Perfectly Packed Suitcase

When all your items are folded, rolled, and in their various
accessories as appropriate, line them up from the heaviest
and largest to the lightest and smallest. Working in complete layers, lay in the largest and heaviest pieces (shoes and
clothes) at the bottom of the suitcase, filling the entire base.
Add in your medium-weight clothes (loungewear, pajamas,
and lightweight tops). Anything you'll need to reach for first
(the outfit you plan to wear when you arrive) should be at
the very top for easy access. Small items that you don't need
right away, like underwear and socks, can be stuffed into the
nooks and crannies of your suitcase. This includes front and
side pouches, if your suitcase has them.

Clothing

Accessories, toiletries,
and beauty

Takeoff
Packing Your In-Flight Bag

Assembling your in-flight bag may be even more important than layering your suitcase, as you'll likely be in and out of it during the trip. I pack the in-flight bag the night before my trip, or in the morning if I have a later flight. (See The Packing Timeline, which starts on page 14.) My in-flight bag includes my iPad or Kindle, laptop, headphones, snacks, and liquids toiletry bag. If it's a long flight (five hours or more), I also pack a neck pillow and eye mask.

If your large bag doesn't have a padded compartment for your laptop or tablet, invest in sleeves and cases for them. These items should also live in your packing station. Your

laptop should be within easy reach in your in-flight bag so you can remove it quickly for security screening.

You've invested in duplicate chargers, so they should be ready to go (see page 33). Wrap the cord around the transformer and secure it with a Velcro electronics tie or hair band to prevent their unraveling and getting tangled. These cords are best off in your in-flight bag, in case you need to recharge your devices while in transit.

You already know you'll be asked for your boarding pass and photo identification when you get to the security checkpoint. Whether it's a passport case and the boarding pass on your phone or a full portfolio with travel confirmations and itineraries, have them ready and consolidated in a travel wallet. Keep it in an outside pocket of your bag for fast access — don't hold it in your hand, lest you put it down somewhere and forget it.

Similarly, you know you'll need to remove your liquid toiletries for screening. Put this bag in your in-flight bag last so it's right at the top, for easy pull-out.

Now you've managed to get yourself succinctly folded, rolled, compartmentalized, zipped, and carried-on. Time to hit the road!

BACKPACKIN'

To help keep a backpack tidy, use two packing cubes. As long as you're willing to wash your clothes, they'll hold enough for five weeks spent abroad.

Come Fly with Me

HOW TO SURVIVE AND THRIVE IN THE AIRPORT AND BEYOND

B y now you've gotten yourself to the airport with time to spare. You're calm, cool, and collected. You look great, like the chic traveler you are. If you think airport security and sitting around at the gate is a drag, just remind yourself that getting to your destination is half the fun. You're well prepared, so let's make the rest of your journey just as perfect. This chapter discusses other things that can likely affect your trip, from others you may be traveling with to staying healthy in flight. It concludes with a discussion of the fine art of unpacking and repacking while away. Shall we?

The Company You Keep
How to Travel with Anyone

Who you travel with influences not just how you pack but also how you travel. These tips will help you pack and travel perfectly, regardless of your travel companions.

TRAVELING WITH COLLEAGUES

For work trips (particularly if you travel with colleagues), you want to bring your professional self with you. Think about what that means to you: proactive, independent, and organized are probably adjectives that come to mind. You're always better off carrying on your suitcase when you are traveling with colleagues; you don't want to be the only one waiting for a checked bag to come down the chute. And make sure you can lift your carry-on suitcase into the overhead compartment with ease, and that your in-flight bag isn't too heavy, either. Practice handling them together.

Wear flats and make sure your travel outfits have a conservative enough neckline and hemline so you don't reveal too much cleavage or leg when you have to bend down or lift up.

If you're going to be renting a car, have the directions pulled up on your phone, and have your car charger/vent clip at the top of your bag before you reach the car rental desk.

TRAVELING WITH FRIENDS

Check in with your companions to see how they're traveling—whether they are doing carry-ons or checked bags. You wouldn't want everyone to have to wait for you to claim your bag if they are all ready to go, right off the plane. You're also going to want to coordinate items that can be borrowed or shared—toiletries, hair tools, and sometimes even clothing.

Be sure everyone has the trip's itinerary, so you can all pack appropriately; there's nothing worse than being underdressed at a fancy dinner or being the only one without a swimsuit.

TRAVELING WITH **YOUR SIGNIFICANT OTHER**

Learn each other's travel quirks as much as you can ahead of time—that is, who prefers to get to the airport early, check-in vs. carry-on preferences, and seat preferences, as well as who is a neat-freak and who might be a bit messy. Compromise and plan accordingly. After you do it a couple of times, the kinks will work themselves out!

Repack the night before you leave, not the day of. On both ends of the trip, last-minute packing can cause stress, which can lead to arguments. Save yourself and your sanity.

TRAVELING WITH **FAMILY**

Assign a project manager for the trip—this person will coordinate who brings what (food, games, beach toys, etc.) and follow up right before the trip to make sure everything has been packed or, alternatively, there is a plan to purchase items when you arrive at your destination.

Bring earplugs, especially if you're traveling with children or babies!

The Express Line
How to Get Through Security Like a Travel Pro

A great airport experience can set the tone for the rest of your trip. These tips will start you off on the right foot.

HAVE EVERYTHING HANDY
Remove your jewelry and belt in the car on the way to the airport. Make sure the items you'll need to remove for screening (laptop, liquids) are packed at the top of your in-flight bag.

WEAR SLIP-ON SHOES
Easy on, easy off. Done.

PICK IT UP, PACK IT LATER
Grab your belongings at the end of security screening and carry them to a nearby bench. Then, and only then, put yourself and your stuff back together. There's nothing worse than clogging the screening table while you assemble your belongings; it inconveniences everyone else. Instead, on the bench, you'll have a calm moment for yourself. Karma is real!

TIME IT RIGHT
If you schedule your flights at off-peak times, you'll avoid major security bottlenecks.

TSA PRECHECK/GLOBAL ENTRY

It's ironic that a big part of traveling is actually standing still, waiting in lines. You may have spotted certain travelers breezing through the security screening, with their shoes on and their laptops in their bags. These folks have signed up for TSA PreCheck, a program that allows them to go through a separate security line without having to remove shoes or jackets and their bag of liquids and laptops still in their suitcases. Global Entry similarly expedites the passport control/customs processes when you return to the United States. Travelers can scan their passports at an electronic kiosk, scan their fingerprint for verification, and complete a customs declaration, instead of waiting in possibly long lines to be processed by an agent. You can find more details and apply for these programs at www.tsa.gov.

Now Boarding
In-Flight Comforts

While most airlines have some sort of on-board entertainment, it may be broken or not to your preference. Before you leave home, take a moment to prep your entertainment—download episodes of your favorite show or movies or music. Make sure all your devices (including a portable battery) are fully charged. A nonelectronic item, whether it's a novel or a puzzle book, is a great backup item. And of course, double-check that your headphones are handy! Between random conversations and crying babies, you'll likely need something to drown out the noise.

Be Well
Stay Healthy in Transit

Travelers often use airports and flights as an excuse to eat badly. Remember that you're not burning many calories when you are sitting on your bum for hours on end. Pre-ordering the strict vegetarian/vegan option is a trick I picked up after years of accepting the standard offerings. The food is usually decent (and vegetable-rich), plus it's served before everyone else's! And don't forget about snacks—especially since most airlines don't serve them as complimentary anymore. I like to bring cut-up veggies and fresh fruit for a mid-flight snack. Definitely avoid bananas and tuna, as their smell can be offensive to your neighbors. Also skip the nuts, as you never know if your row mates are allergic.

Once you've ensured you'll be well fed en route, work on staying healthy during the trip. Planes are incubators for viruses. After you board, wipe down your arm rests, your seat belt fasteners, tray table, window pull, and even the wall next to your seat with sanitizing towels. Add vitamin packs to your water for an extra boost, and always use a paper towel to open the bathroom door from the inside as you are leaving. Don't use the water in the bathroom to brush your teeth, as the containers that hold the water aren't cleaned frequently and carry a lot of bacteria. Use a bottle of water or waterless toothbrushes instead.

I don't recommend drinking in transit, but if you do, opt for a glass of red wine or a Bloody Mary. Ideally, you should drink plenty of water because flying is dehydrating. I recommend a cup of herbal tea as the best way to lull yourself to sleep. Use the airline-provided pillow for lower back support, a neck pillow to cradle your head, and steeped chamomile teabags (wrapped in tissues) as compresses for your eyes before slipping on a silk eye mask. The skin under your eyes is the most delicate, and these steps will significantly help keep it hydrated in flight. For many busy travelers, flights are the only acceptable time to be disconnected from others and relax.

OH NO! MY LUGGAGE IS LOST!

First, be assured that less than 1 percent of passengers' luggage gets lost—so this is an unlikely scenario. To err on the side of caution, take a picture of your suitcase in case they lose it, so you can provide specifics for the search. But don't panic! You have everything you'll need for the next 24 hours in your in-flight bag.

Stay calm, and don't feel that you need to immediately go out and buy new things. Chances are your suitcase will turn up. If it's just the typical lost luggage snag, your belongings will likely be sent to you within 48 hours. If the loss is due to inclement weather, though, it could take up to a week to recover the bag.

There's always the chance someone has taken your checked bag by mistake. If you include a GPS tracking tile in your luggage, it will help in locating the person. However, anything you carry on the plane is under your control. Be sure to inspect your entire seating area before you de-plane. Electronics in the seat pockets are most commonly left behind.

We Are Arriving at Your Destination

IF YOU ARRIVE IN THE MORNING
Try to stay awake as long as possible. Get lots of sun and natural light to send signals to your body that it is daytime. Change your clothes and break a sweat. You don't need to go straight to the hotel gym, but be active. That *doesn't* mean you should plan a big activity for the moment you arrive. Instead, explore the neighborhood and get to know your surroundings. If you really need to sleep during that first day, take a short nap only after lunch. Don't eat anything heavy when you arrive, because your body is still in inactive mode. Try to find a green juice or order some vegetables to reset your body with nutrients.

IF YOU ARRIVE AT NIGHT
Don't overstimulate yourself. Try to follow your usual nighttime routine even though it might be day where you came from. Take a hot shower to relax. Unpacking late at night might be too much activity, so be sure to have your pajamas on top for easy reach and then unpack in the morning. Stay away from bright lights and screens—read a book instead. Melatonin can help you induce sleep when you might not naturally be tired, but ask your doctor before taking any medications.

DEALING WITH JET LAG

Jet lag happens. It's a drag, but there are things you can do to make it much better. If you can, choose a flight during which you'd be sleeping at the time zone of your destination. But remember that flight time and sleep time are not the same. Deduct at least 90 minutes for takeoff and landing from your total sleep time—so a six-hour flight would give you about four and a half hours of sleep. Also, try to time your exposure to light with how it appears at your destination, so you can start to reset your circadian rhythm: dim the lights, wear your eye mask, or put on sunglasses. If you must be awake and looking at a screen, dimming it to the lowest setting can help you readjust.

How to Unpack

STEP 1: Create a checklist of items you're going to remove from your bag and use in your room. Bring along your filled-out packing list as a reference, and note where you unpacked your various items (clothes in the closet and dresser, valuables in the safe). In addition to your clothes and toiletries, make note of your electronics, valuables, and identification.

STEP 2: Remove your clothes from your suitcase, hanging them up and placing them in drawers. Remove your toiletries and arrange them in the bathroom.

STEP 3: Set up a spot for your laundry bag.

STEP 4: Transfer your valuables to the hotel safe or, barring that, a discreet, secure location inside your suitcase.

STEP 5: Go enjoy your trip!

If you're staying only for a day or two, or are hopping from city to city, there are a couple of tweaks to that checklist. When you take your clothes out of your bag, roll your outfits according to each day you're wearing them. Return items to your toiletry bags as you use them.

The Long Goodbye
Ending Your Trip Right

How you end a trip is just as important as how you begin it. You've got to repack perfectly, too! The goal is to reassemble your bag as closely as you can to how it was before. Whether you're prone to leaving items behind or are more interested in savoring the last minutes of your trip, this method of repacking will help. It's fast and it's organized.

The first thing to go in should be your laundry bag—it will take up the most space. Anything that's not dirty, you should refold, reroll, recube, and repack.

Remember that checklist you made when you got here? Pull it out and start ticking everything off. Before you zip up your bag, check inside the shower, under the bed, inside the nightstands, in the safe, and at the plug points.

Tip your housekeeper, and be on your way. Leave time to take one final walk around your hotel. Don't take pictures. Don't listen to music. Just look around. This is why you came here. To *see* things.

Back at Home Base

Believe it or not, as soon as you're back at the ranch you can begin preparing for your next journey. Toss the contents of your laundry bag into your hamper (or better yet, straight into your washing machine). Restock your toiletry bags so you're prepared for your next trip. Back up the pictures and videos you snapped on your phone, and even order a new print to decorate your packing station.

Examine your packing list to see if you used every item you packed. Erase or cross off what you didn't wear or use. Chances are, you won't need it next time and can use that space for something else. And on the flip side, add anything you wish you'd brought along on this trip.

If you've been on a business trip, scan your receipts and save the information for any new business contacts. Jot down some notes to share with your team. If you were on an adventure trip, why not schedule a massage? Check if any of your gear needs to be revamped or refurbished, so it's ready for next time. And if you're just back from vacation—start thinking about where you want to visit next.

Reflect on the trip you just took: How did it change you? What did you discover about yourself? The pack-perfect principles exist so you're free to focus on your adventure and on the new experiences, rather than on your stuff. You can marvel, wander, or nail a job interview with ease when you're not worried about your belongings. If *you are what you pack*, then ask yourself: Were you the person you wanted to be on this trip? I hope so!

Acknowledgments

Kim Perel—where do I even begin? You are the fairy godmother of this book. There are no words in any of the world's languages (and some fictional ones) to express how much I love you and the work you put into this book and me. I'm grateful to call you my agent, my cowriter, and most important, my dear friend.

Kelly Lasserre, your illustrations breathed life into this book. You make packing, something that's typically messy and frantic, look absolutely beautiful. Thank you for bringing your talent and your warm spirit to this book.

Lisa Tauber, I will never forget how I felt when I received that first email from you, asking if I ever thought about writing a book. This book wouldn't exist without you. Thank you for seeing something that I didn't. Amanda Englander, how you managed to shepherd this book through the tight deadlines and my complete lack of experience is beyond me. Thank you for bringing this book to life.

Taking on this book on the heels of having a baby and launching a business was, in hindsight, insane. It also would have been impossible without my village. Mom and Dad—you always taught me to go after my dreams. I can never thank you enough for how you dropped everything to take care of Rho and me while I chased my dreams. To my husband—if there's anything I've learned in the year I worked on this book, it's that marrying you was the best decision I ever made. Thank you for your endless support, pep talks, and for the perfect cup of tea every morning. Samira—my work wife, my sister, my best friend. Thank you for carrying the B2A load when I needed to buckle down on the book, for our countless couch wine and work sessions, and for your constant support and love. Naleeni—I can't remember my life before you, and I never want to. Thank you for loving and caring for my son the way you do. To my in-laws—thank you for welcoming me into your family and for all your support.

To my friends who rode my emotional roller coaster with endless support—thank you for the impromptu video chats, the frantic phone calls, and for meeting me at Hillstone's when I needed it. You know you who are, and I can't thank you enough. But that won't stop me from trying.

Thank you, Hillstone's, for your excellent spinach dip, dirty martinis, and sushi—aka my writing fuel.

To my Hitha On The Go family—there would be no book or blog without *you*. Thank you for your generous time, comments, messages, and shares of my little corner of the Internet. You are the reason I keep writing and creating. Thank you, thank you, thank you.

And finally, to Rho. You are the best part of my life.

ABOUT THE AUTHOR

Hitha Palepu is an entrepreneur and a writer with extensive global experience in the life sciences, travel, and technology fields. She is the founder of Hitha On The Go, a lifestyle website founded in 2009 focused on helping women live their best lives.

Hitha currently serves as the cofounder and chief operating officer of Bridge2Act, a start-up technology company enabling charitable giving in a rapid, easy, and more informed manner. The company launched NO.GIFTS, a platform for people to "gift" their special days to amazing causes.

Prior to founding Bridge2Act, Hitha served as vice president, Business Development, for SciDose, a research-focused pharmaceutical company specializing in developing enhanced formulations for existing oncology and hospital injectable products. She was responsible for worldwide licensing of the SciDose portfolio and closed numerous deals totaling over $300 million in several diverse geographic areas.

Hitha graduated from the University of Washington with degrees in biochemistry and history. She lives in New York with her husband and son.

PACKING LIST

Destination: _____

Length of Trip: _____

Weather Report: _____

OUTFITS

Day 1	Day 2	Day 3	Day 4	Day 5
AM	AM	AM	AM	AM
PM	PM	PM	PM	PM

CLOTHING

Tops	Bottoms	Dresses
1.	1.	1.
2.	2.	2.
3.	3.	3.
4.	4.	4.
5.	5.	5.

Underwear	Pajamas/Lounge	Workout
_____ underpants	_____ pajamas	_____ workout pants
_____ bras	_____ lounge outfit	_____ workout tops
_____ socks	_____ robe	_____ sports bras
shapewear:		

SHOES

BAGS

OTHER ACCESSORIES

- [ ] Sunglasses
- [ ] Scarf
- [ ] Hat
- [ ] Belt
- [ ] Jewelry

TOILETRIES

- [ ] Liquids
- [ ] Non-Liquids
- [ ] Beauty

ELECTRONICS

- [ ] Laptop
- [ ] Tablet
- [ ] Phone
- [ ] Charger
- [ ] Charger
- [ ] Charger
- [ ] Headphones

PACKING LIST

Destination: _____

Length of Trip: _____

Weather Report: _____

OUTFITS

Day 1	Day 2	Day 3	Day 4	Day 5
AM	AM	AM	AM	AM
PM	PM	PM	PM	PM

CLOTHING

Tops	Bottoms	Dresses
1.	1.	1.
2.	2.	2.
3.	3.	3.
4.	4.	4.
5.	5.	5.

Underwear	Pajamas/Lounge	Workout
_____ underpants	_____ pajamas	_____ workout pants
_____ bras	_____ lounge outfit	_____ workout tops
_____ socks	_____ robe	_____ sports bras
shapewear:		

SHOES

BAGS

OTHER ACCESSORIES

☐ Sunglasses ☐ Scarf ☐ Hat

☐ Belt ☐ Jewelry

TOILETRIES

☐ Liquids ☐ Non-Liquids ☐ Beauty

ELECTRONICS

☐ Laptop ☐ Tablet ☐ Phone

☐ Charger ☐ Charger ☐ Charger

☐ Headphones

PACKING LIST

Destination: _____

Length of Trip: _____

Weather Report: _____

OUTFITS

Day 1	Day 2	Day 3	Day 4	Day 5
AM	AM	AM	AM	AM
PM	PM	PM	PM	PM

CLOTHING

Tops	Bottoms	Dresses
1.	1.	1.
2.	2.	2.
3.	3.	3.
4.	4.	4.
5.	5.	5.

Underwear	Pajamas/Lounge	Workout
_____ underpants	_____ pajamas	_____ workout pants
_____ bras	_____ lounge outfit	_____ workout tops
_____ socks	_____ robe	_____ sports bras
shapewear:		

SHOES

BAGS

OTHER ACCESSORIES

- ☐ Sunglasses
- ☐ Scarf
- ☐ Hat
- ☐ Belt
- ☐ Jewelry

TOILETRIES

- ☐ Liquids
- ☐ Non-Liquids
- ☐ Beauty

ELECTRONICS

- ☐ Laptop
- ☐ Tablet
- ☐ Phone
- ☐ Charger
- ☐ Charger
- ☐ Charger
- ☐ Headphones

PACKING LIST

Destination: _____

Length of Trip: _____

Weather Report: _____

OUTFITS

Day 1	Day 2	Day 3	Day 4	Day 5
AM	AM	AM	AM	AM
PM	PM	PM	PM	PM

CLOTHING

Tops	Bottoms	Dresses
1.	1.	1.
2.	2.	2.
3.	3.	3.
4.	4.	4.
5.	5.	5.

Underwear	Pajamas/Lounge	Workout
_____ underpants	_____ pajamas	_____ workout pants
_____ bras	_____ lounge outfit	_____ workout tops
_____ socks	_____ robe	_____ sports bras
shapewear:		

SHOES

BAGS

OTHER ACCESSORIES

- ☐ Sunglasses
- ☐ Scarf
- ☐ Hat
- ☐ Belt
- ☐ Jewelry

TOILETRIES

- ☐ Liquids
- ☐ Non-Liquids
- ☐ Beauty

ELECTRONICS

- ☐ Laptop
- ☐ Tablet
- ☐ Phone
- ☐ Charger
- ☐ Charger
- ☐ Charger
- ☐ Headphones

PACKING LIST

Destination: _____

Length of Trip: _____

Weather Report: _____

OUTFITS

Day 1	Day 2	Day 3	Day 4	Day 5
AM	AM	AM	AM	AM
PM	PM	PM	PM	PM

CLOTHING

Tops	Bottoms	Dresses
1.	1.	1.
2.	2.	2.
3.	3.	3.
4.	4.	4.
5.	5.	5.

Underwear	Pajamas/Lounge	Workout
_____ underpants	_____ pajamas	_____ workout pants
_____ bras	_____ lounge outfit	_____ workout tops
_____ socks	_____ robe	_____ sports bras
shapewear:		

SHOES

BAGS

OTHER ACCESSORIES

☐ Sunglasses ☐ Scarf ☐ Hat

☐ Belt ☐ Jewelry

TOILETRIES

☐ Liquids ☐ Non-Liquids ☐ Beauty

ELECTRONICS

☐ Laptop ☐ Tablet ☐ Phone

☐ Charger ☐ Charger ☐ Charger

☐ Headphones

PACKING LIST

Destination: _____

Length of Trip: _____

Weather Report: _____

OUTFITS

Day 1	Day 2	Day 3	Day 4	Day 5
AM	AM	AM	AM	AM
PM	PM	PM	PM	PM

CLOTHING

Tops	Bottoms	Dresses
1.	1.	1.
2.	2.	2.
3.	3.	3.
4.	4.	4.
5.	5.	5.

Underwear	Pajamas/Lounge	Workout
_____ underpants	_____ pajamas	_____ workout pants
_____ bras	_____ lounge outfit	_____ workout tops
_____ socks	_____ robe	_____ sports bras
shapewear:		

SHOES

BAGS

OTHER ACCESSORIES

- ☐ Sunglasses
- ☐ Belt
- ☐ Scarf
- ☐ Jewelry
- ☐ Hat

TOILETRIES

- ☐ Liquids
- ☐ Non-Liquids
- ☐ Beauty

ELECTRONICS

- ☐ Laptop
- ☐ Charger
- ☐ Headphones
- ☐ Tablet
- ☐ Charger
- ☐ Phone
- ☐ Charger

PACKING LIST

Destination: _____

Length of Trip: _____

Weather Report: _____

OUTFITS

Day 1	Day 2	Day 3	Day 4	Day 5
AM	AM	AM	AM	AM
PM	PM	PM	PM	PM

CLOTHING

Tops	*Bottoms*	*Dresses*
1.	1.	1.
2.	2.	2.
3.	3.	3.
4.	4.	4.
5.	5.	5.

Underwear	*Pajamas/Lounge*	*Workout*
_____ underpants	_____ pajamas	_____ workout pants
_____ bras	_____ lounge outfit	_____ workout tops
_____ socks	_____ robe	_____ sports bras
shapewear:		

SHOES

BAGS

OTHER ACCESSORIES

- ☐ Sunglasses
- ☐ Belt
- ☐ Scarf
- ☐ Jewelry
- ☐ Hat

TOILETRIES

- ☐ Liquids
- ☐ Non-Liquids
- ☐ Beauty

ELECTRONICS

- ☐ Laptop
- ☐ Charger
- ☐ Headphones
- ☐ Tablet
- ☐ Charger
- ☐ Phone
- ☐ Charger

PACKING LIST

Destination: _____

Length of Trip: _____

Weather Report: _____

OUTFITS

Day 1	Day 2	Day 3	Day 4	Day 5
AM	AM	AM	AM	AM
PM	PM	PM	PM	PM

CLOTHING

Tops	Bottoms	Dresses
1.	1.	1.
2.	2.	2.
3.	3.	3.
4.	4.	4.
5.	5.	5.

Underwear	Pajamas/Lounge	Workout
_____ underpants	_____ pajamas	_____ workout pants
_____ bras	_____ lounge outfit	_____ workout tops
_____ socks	_____ robe	_____ sports bras
shapewear:		

SHOES

BAGS

OTHER ACCESSORIES

- ☐ Sunglasses
- ☐ Scarf
- ☐ Hat
- ☐ Belt
- ☐ Jewelry

TOILETRIES

- ☐ Liquids
- ☐ Non-Liquids
- ☐ Beauty

ELECTRONICS

- ☐ Laptop
- ☐ Tablet
- ☐ Phone
- ☐ Charger
- ☐ Charger
- ☐ Charger
- ☐ Headphones